World Population
Still the biggest problem?

World population is now 6.4 billion, compared with 2.5 billion in 1950 (and 1 billion in 1830). By 2050, total population seems likely to reach 9 billion. Over 90% of this growth will take place in developing countries, many of which have serious social, economic and environmental problems.

Some are seeing rapid economic growth and becoming massive new consumer societies. What are the implications of the continuing growth in world population?

Other titles in this series

In preparation

UGI Report no. 122

World Population
Still the biggest problem?

Understanding **Global Issues**

World Population:
Still the biggest problem?

Editor: Richard Buckley

Published by
Understanding Global Issues Limited,
The Runnings, Cheltenham GL51 9PQ, England

Artwork: The Chapman Partnership

Cover: Jonathan Chapman

Photographs:
Associated Press: p.28;
Richard and Ben Buckley: p.29, p.42, p.44,
p.45, p.46

ISBN 085233 001 4

Printed in the UK by The Alden Group, Oxford

Contents

Introduction

No-one knows how many people the planet can
support, though concerns about food supplies and
environmental damage have grown as population has
soared from 2 billion in 1930 to 6.4 billion in 2004. Further
growth to 9 billion seems likely by mid-century, though
earlier predictions of 12 billion now seem exaggerated
because fertility rates (the average number of children per
woman) have fallen much more quickly than expected.

The doomsday predictions commonly made in the 1980s
have not, so far, been borne out by events. Famines have
occurred but not on the massive scale forecast. It has
become fashionable to argue that neo-Malthusian[1] panic
is overdone. After all, say the optimists, most people are
healthier and living longer than ever before; environmental
degradation is manageable; biotech will ensure there is
plenty of food for everyone; poverty is the real problem and

the main effort should be devoted to helping economies in the South become more like those in the North.

Even the optimists have to recognise that the challenges are daunting. Hunger afflicts a billion of the world's poor; expansion of global food supply is being made harder by water scarcity and soil degradation; per capita cropland falls as population grows; the need to force the soil to produce even higher yields in the future could accelerate the process of environmental damage; genetic engineering may help with food supply but probably not within the timeframe needed.

Far from getting narrower, the gap between 'haves' and 'have-nots' is widening. According to the UN's *Human Development Report 2002*, the world's richest 1% of people receive as much income as the poorest 57%. The disparity between richest and poorest has doubled since 1960. The developed countries show little inclination to distribute their wealth among the poor or to curb their own extravagant lifestyles. Even small steps in this direction, such as increasing foreign aid or putting taxes on energy use, are nettles too uncomfortable for most politicians to grasp – and voters to accept. Meanwhile, the vast army of urban poor in the developing world continues to grow, increasing the dangers of social unrest and aggressive international migration. About 1.2 billion people live on less than $1 a day, and 1.7 billion live in countries facing water stress. Population growth often exacerbates these problems. The environment is affected not only by numbers but also by behaviour. After all, the 20% of people who live in the developed world are reckoned to account for 80% of global pollution and resource use.

Additions to the human race are currently running at over 75 million people a year. About 95% of this growth is taking place in the developing countries of the world, countries which are already struggling to provide a decent standard of living for their existing populations. There is a strong link between population growth and improvements in living standards. For example, South Korea and Ethiopia had roughly similar rates of poverty and population growth in 1950. South Korea, which has given a high priority to education and family planning, has dramatically improved the living standards of its people, while reducing fertility rates from over 6 in 1950 to 1.4 in 2003. Gross national income per head at purchasing power parity (PPP) was $17,930 in South Korea in 2003 – compared to $710 in Ethiopia where the fertility rate was 6.4. Ethiopia's population, 18 million in 1950, is now over 65 million and forecast to reach 171 million by 2050.

By contrast Europe's population is expected to fall by almost 100 million by 2050. Over the same time period, population in Africa is forecast to grow by almost a billion and in Asia by 1.4 billion. The pressure to migrate to Europe will be immense.

Attempts to impose 'number-driven' population control programmes have proved counter-productive. For example, compulsory sterilisation in the 1970s gave family planning a bad name in India and set back the whole effort to limit population growth in that country. Preoccupation with the difficult moral issue of abortion[2] has also undermined public support for population programmes. Yet lack of access to contraception *increases* the number of abortions, just as lack of sex education for teenagers results in more unwanted births and sexually transmitted disease.

Delegates at the International Conference on Population and Development in Cairo in 1994 agreed a 20-year action plan to tackle the population problem. Countries agreed to spend some $17bn a year on population and reproductive health, with about one-third of this sum provided by the developed world and two-thirds by developing countries. In recent years, however, the richer countries have provided only half of their $6bn a year commitment, leaving a $3bn funding gap. This shortfall is making it harder to achieve development goals and could mean that world population in 2050 will be well above the 9 billion currently predicted. The UN's 20-year plan, now at the halfway stage, involves a complex mixture of solutions involving education, gender equality, health care, sustainable economic development and family planning. Most basic of all is a woman's right to decide how many children to bear – a right taken for granted in industrialised countries but still all too rare in the developing world.

As fertility rates have fallen, the sense of urgency about population control that used to be common in the early 1990s has been reduced. In the West, population decline and ageing have made large families seem more acceptable. Meanwhile, high fertility rates continue in many developing countries and the presence of over a billion sexually mature adolescents in the world ensures that population will continue to grow strongly. Indeed it could surge well beyond the UN prediction of 8.9 billion by 2050 if efforts to provide universal access to contraception begin to flag for lack of political support, especially from the US.

After his election in 2000, President George W. Bush showed that he was close to the Christian Coalition position on population issues, seeing attempts to control fertility as an infringement of human rights and vigorously opposing the inclusion of abortion in reproductive health services. One of the first acts of the Bush administration was to reduce US funding for the UN Population Fund (UNFPA), the world's largest international source of funding for population and reproductive health programmes. The UNFPA, working closely with governments and NGOs, helps to provide contraceptives, family planning advice and services to support safe pregnancy and childbirth throughout the developing world.

Leaving aside the question of total population and the planet's carrying capacity, it is surely a fundamental human right for women to be able to choose how many children they want and to give birth safely. Only modern contraception and health care can bring this about.

1 A 20th Century Explosion

For most of human history, population grew very slowly. In recent years, it has exploded as higher standards of health and nutrition have spread around the world.

Homo proliferans – the Malthusian nightmare

All species strive to proliferate, but predators, disease and starvation limit populations which get out of hand and disturb the balance of nature. Can humanity keep its population in check before nature applies its own brutal methods?

In 10,000 BCE, the total population of the world was about six million, probably the sustainable maximum at a time when human beings had to rely on hunting and gathering in order to survive. Extinction was a real possibility as humans fought with the elements and with other animals to keep their species alive. Life expectancy was only about 20 years and birth rates were only marginally above death rates. At that time, man's grip on life was precarious and his impact on the natural environment was negligible.

As settled agriculture and weaponry developed, human beings were able to produce food more easily and to defend themselves more readily. The result was to increase their life expectancy and prolong the years of potential parenthood, leading to growth in population. Nevertheless, in mid-18th century Europe, the total population of about 100 million was probably all that could be sustained by contemporary agriculture.

Even when world population was less than half a billion, human activity had transformed the landscape, in particular by cutting down trees to clear land for farming and to provide wood for fuel and building materials.

The explosive growth of world population is a recent phenomenon, with the 20th century alone accounting for 75% of all population growth that has taken place in the last 12,000 years.

Population in the first decade of the 21st century is growing at some 75 million people a year. Feeding, housing and employing them presents human society with a massive problem.

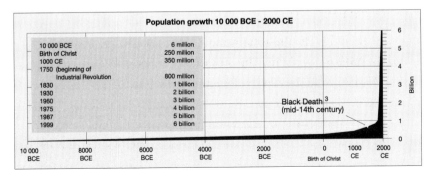

Population growth 10 000 BCE - 2000 CE

10 000 BCE	6 million
Birth of Christ	250 million
1000 CE	350 million
1750 (beginning of Industrial Revolution	800 million
1830	1 billion
1930	2 billion
1960	3 billion
1975	4 billion
1987	5 billion
1999	6 billion

Black Death [3]
(mid-14th century)

Annual population growth between the year 1000 and 1750 was only about 0.1%. By 1750 average life expectancy was still only 27 years. Half of newborn babies died before reaching the age of five. Although fertility was high, famines, disease and war prevented the population from expanding.

The Industrial Revolution changed the technology of food production and enabled a much larger population to be supported. At the same time, improvements in health care reduced infant mortality and enabled people to live much longer lives. By the early 1960s, world population was growing at 2% a year, adding 70 million people annually. As the base population expanded, the total added each year grew to 90 million in the early 1990s. Though average fertility has fallen in the last decade and annual population growth has fallen to 1.3%, population is still growing by 75 million people each year.

2 Population's Momentum

Even a small difference between birth rates and death rates can make a big difference to population. An annual natural increase of 1% doubles population in 67 years.

Propagation of the species is a natural imperative

All animals are driven by the instinct to reproduce. For most human beings living in educated, affluent society, the sexual act has become separated from its reproductive function by contraception. Women can make their own choices about the number of children they want, and most opt for small families. Indeed, population in the industrialised world has started to decline.

In much of the developing world, however, couples still prefer the security of larger families. Women often have little or no chance to practise family planning, even if they want it. At the same time, improved medical care has reduced death rates. The result is that births outrun deaths and population is growing rapidly.

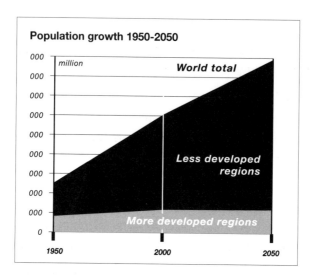

The population of a country depends on three main factors – birth rate, death rate and migration. Migration has always been important in determining local population.

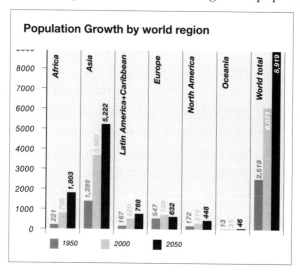

Mass migrations are taking place in many parts of the world and will profoundly affect the size and nature of countries. However, migration has no effect on total world population.

In the crudest terms, population growth or decline depends on the difference between births and deaths. A small imbalance rapidly leads to large changes in population.

The difference between a rapidly growing population and a stable population is only a few percentage points. For example, if the natural increase (i.e., the difference between birth and death rates) is 0.1%, as it is in the UK, it takes over a thousand years for the population to double. If the annual rate of natural increase is 1%, the population doubles in about 67 years. If the rate is 2.9%, as in Central Africa, the doubling time is only 24 years.

The basic reason why population has rocketed during the last century is that a steep decline in death rates has not been accompanied by a similar decline in birth rates. Human beings have escaped the natural limitations of the wild, where weaker young animals die in their millions in a grisly 'survival of the fittest'. However, some prophets of doom see mass annihilation of human beings through famine, pestilence or war as the inevitable outcome of our failure to take the population issue seriously enough.

If women had children to the limit of their biological potential, they would have as many as 20 children each. In fact, they have far fewer even in countries where child-bearing is encouraged. Clearly there are strong cultural factors which limit human reproduction. The age at which marriage takes place, religious belief, local custom and economic pressure all have a part to play.

One of the most important considerations is child health. If a substantial number of the children borne by a woman are likely to die before reaching adulthood, a mother will tend to have more pregnancies than if her children are normally expected to grow up healthy. Worldwide, 5.5% of babies die within the first year of life, but there are huge variations from place to place. The rate is 20% in Mozambique, less than 1% in Western Europe.

Improved health care

Even a small surplus of birth rates over death rates results in rapid population growth. Improved health care saw average death rates fall dramatically in the 20th century.

In developed countries, modern contraception is readily available and well understood by most women. On the whole, western women get pregnant only when they want to. Reproductive freedom is one of the most important human rights gained by women in the developed world. It is not, however, a freedom enjoyed by women in poorer countries, where cultural expectations and lack of contraception oblige many women to have one pregnancy after another. About 11% of all births are to teenagers, yet adolescents are frequently excluded from family planning and sex education programmes run by government.

If contraception is unavailable or not used, unwanted pregnancies are inevitable. Do women have a right to

Infant mortality

For most of human history, a high death rate among children was regarded as inevitable, and dying in childbirth was common for women. In 19th century Britain, large families were the norm – Queen Victoria herself had nine children (though she loathed her pregnancies). What was unusual was that all her children survived. Though family planning tends to get most attention when population issues are discussed today, health care is just as important. Improvements in the medical care provided to mothers and children have resulted in a dramatic decline in infant mortality and childbirth deaths. The downside of this human development progress has been to accelerate population growth.

Infant deaths per 1,000 live births

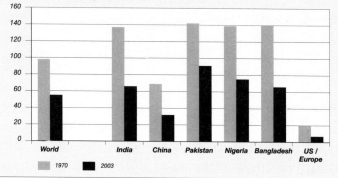

abort an unwanted foetus? At what point does a human life begin? At the point of conception? When the foetus becomes recognisably human? At the actual birth? Dealing with such issues is not for the squeamish and can be political dynamite.

Worldwide, some 900,000 conceptions occur each day, with at least half being unplanned and probably a quarter unwanted. Some 20% of pregnancies fail spontaneously, usually during the early months. Induced abortions are common in many societies, with some 150,000 being performed each day around the world. The lowest rate of abortion is in the Netherlands, where contraception and sex education are widely promoted.

Medical care is a key factor in the population issue. Not only has it reduced infant deaths, but it has also ensured that more and more people live into old age. In 1800, average life expectancy in Europe was about 35 years. By 1900 it was about 50 years and today about 75 years. In developing countries, life expectancy was about 40 in 1950 and today has risen to over 60, though there are wide variations from country to country. Even in affluent societies, looking after old people is becoming a serious social problem. Poorer countries will have a far worse problem when their populations age.

All this has been accompanied by a dramatic shift from rural to urban living. For thousands of years, most of the world's population has lived in the countryside. By 2025 almost two-thirds of the world's population will live in urban areas.

3 An Overloaded Planet

Views differ on how many people the planet can support. A larger population is bound to affect the environment, though the relationship is by no means clearcut.

Environmental degradation – the key national security issue of the future?

With the end of the Cold War, the world has become more chaotic. Ethnic and religious conflict, 'warlords' and terrorism are recognised problems. But future wars may well be provoked by scarcity or degradation of natural resources – land, water, minerals, and even clean air.

The impact of population growth on the environment is not clearcut. In new frontier regions, where people are clearing jungle for farmland or cutting down forest on hillsides, there is obvious damage to the environment. In most countries, the best cropland and most suitable settlement areas are already occupied, so that further expansion has to take place in marginal areas where ecosystems are fragile and environmental damage is likely to be high.

Ecological footprints

'Ecological footprinting' attempts to quantify the impact of human consumption on the environment. The best-known method of measuring the footprint was developed by Mathis Wackernagel and Dr William Rees, and was used in the WWF's *Living Planet Report 2002*. The report's conclusion was that human consumption already outruns

By region and income group 1999

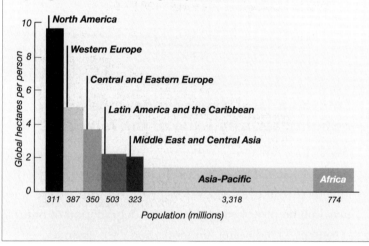

In the last 50 years global deforestation has amounted to almost 10 million sq km as farmland and settlements have been extended. In many parts of Sub-Saharan Africa the demand for fuelwood regularly outruns the renewal of tree stocks. Since 1950 Africa has lost some 2.6 million sq km of forest and woodland – an area as big as Argentina. However, even more damage can be caused by consumer demand in the earth's biological capacity by some 20% – and would be over three times biocapacity if everyone on the planet consumed at the rate of people in the high income countries. North America and Western Europe have the biggest 'footprints', with Americans estimated to use 10 'global hectares' per person (against a world average of about 2 ha).

World ecological footprint 1961 - 99

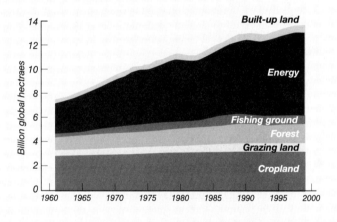

the rich world. The impact on rainforest destruction of, for example, the fast-food industry (which has cleared forest for cattle pasture) and the timber industry (which offers its customers hardwood products) has been well documented.

Increasing affluence may bring consumer pressure for conservation, especially at local level where damage is most visible. Thus Japanese forests have been conserved by placing two-thirds of them under public ownership. Consumer pressure is less intense when it comes to protecting the environment in someone else's country. Japanese customers remain heavy buyers of tropical timber.

Consumer societies all over the world are increasing in size and making ever more heavy demands on natural resources. Known reserves of oil and important minerals have increased in recent years as exploration and extraction techniques have improved. However, it cannot be assumed that supplies are inexhaustible, especially if everyone consumes at North American levels. Human ingenuity is good at finding substitutes for materials which become expensive because of scarce supply. But can scientists provide 'technological fixes'

Water – is there enough for nine billion people?

Water is a key factor in the ability of a region to cope with rapidly increasing population. But water is only one of the many environmental constraints on population growth.

quickly enough as the time for adaptation is squeezed by rapid population growth and accelerating consumer demand?

In any case, science cannot provide substitutes for air and water. Two billion people in 80 countries already live in areas affected by water shortages. As population grows, water scarcity in arid regions is expected to increase tenfold in the next few decades. Moreover, the quality of water in both developed and developing countries is deteriorating because of pollution.

Greenhouse gases continue to accumulate in the atmosphere, increasing the dangers of climate change. Stabilising their concentrations would require an immediate cut of 60% in worldwide emissions of carbon dioxide, the main greenhouse gas. Yet the burning of fossil fuels (which creates carbon dioxide) is increasing with population growth and improved standards of living. Meanwhile, despite much tougher environmental laws, industries in all too many countries continue to release into the environment large amounts of toxic chemicals, heavy metals and acidic gases.

The world's population of motor vehicles (over 700 million in 2003) is growing at some 50 million new cars a year. Demand for private cars in China and India is increasing as economic development proceeds. The impact of this rapid increase in cars threatens to overwhelm attempts to reduce global carbon dioxide emissions. Though car technology has greatly improved, a mass market in emissions-free vehicles is a future dream not current reality.

In the developing world, the population of urban centres is growing twice as fast as total population, because of widespread migration to cities. This is putting enormous strains on services such as sewerage, water, electricity and health care. The biggest increases in urban conglomeration are taking place in the developing world. By 2015 cities such as Dhaka, Mumbai, São Paulo and Delhi will each have over 20m inhabitants. Air quality in such cities is often a danger to health.

Fertile soil is another vital resource which is being depleted. Experts attending the 12th International Soil Conservation Organisation conference in May 2002 were told that 65% of global soil showed signs of degradation. Problems include erosion, salinisation, contamination, waterlogging, compaction, desertification and loss of soil fertility. Because most human settlements begin in areas where land is most fertile, urbanisation often results in concreting over the best farmland.

Loss of biodiversity[4] is accelerating, with species disappearing for ever at the rate of thousands a year. Almost half of all flowering plants live in areas that are likely to be deforested or disturbed over the next 30 years. Habitat loss, the major cause of species destruction, is usually caused by expanding human settlement or consumer pressure on natural resources.

4 Sustainable Development

What would happen if everyone on the planet adopted the consumer tastes of Americans and Europeans? Could the earth survive the onslaught on its resources?

Extravagance and poverty

The world faces a terrible dilemma – how to bring economic improvement to billions of people in the developing world, without destroying the quality of life of everyone on the planet. Despite new emphasis on pollution control and renewable energy, environmental degradation continues to grow.

In recent years awareness of environmental issues has grown enormously in the rich world, but old habits die hard. Though consumer pressure is forcing companies to invent less wasteful manufacturing processes and use fewer toxic substances, the green revolution is taking place only slowly. It will be many years before even the most progressive countries stop polluting the environment. Their efforts could be swamped by increases in pollution from newly industrialising countries, whose populations are anxious to catch up with the developed world. At the global level, growing consumerism may overwhelm the slow movement towards sustainable development.

Human societies can be remarkably adaptive, but whether they can switch to sustainable ways of living quickly enough to prevent serious damage to the planet remains to be seen. Another three billion people – the likely outcome of population growth by 2050 – will make the task of adaptation much harder. At present the world's population is split more or less 50:50 between rural and urban, but the proportion of city dwellers is growing rapidly. According to

Guess which consumers have more impact on the environment. Though people in the developed world account for only a fifth of world population, they cause 80% of global pollution and resource depletion.

the 2003 revision of the periodic UN report *World Urbanis-ation Prospects*, some 5bn people will be living in towns and cities by 2030, when world population is expected to be about 8.1bn. As the proportion of urban dwellers increases, so the number of families living from subsistence agriculture is reduced. Yet these families still have to eat. The inevitable result will be greater use of large-scale intensive farming.

Another aspect of urbanisation is a weakening of the link between people and their understanding of the natural world. Children who grow up in cities, though better educated than their rural counterparts, lack first-hand experience of the importance of water, soil fertility, climate change and biodiversity.

From a commercial point of view, a larger population means a bigger market and a source of cheaper labour. In recent years, nothing has excited the multinationals as much as

the opening up of China and other Asian markets. But the attraction lies in the prospective buying power of these new customers rather than in their numbers. Population is growing fastest in Africa but far more businessmen are flying to Beijing, Jakarta and Bangkok than to Lagos and Abidjan.

Better living standards, bigger environmental impact

A typical American consumes 50 times as much as an average Kenyan – and does far more damage to the global ecosystem. Because they live mostly in cities, consumers are often unaware of the harm they are causing in the natural world.

Some Asian countries with high economic growth have managed to reduce fertility rates close to replacement level (roughly 2.1 children per mother). Examples include Japan (1.3), South Korea (1.4), Thailand (1.9) and China (1.8) – all of which have well-educated populations and effective family planning programmes. In most cases, however, their populations will keep growing until the age structure becomes evenly balanced. China alone is expected to have nearly 1.5 billion people by 2025 – but at least demographic transition[5] is underway. In Japan, a mature economy where living standards have been high for many years, population is expected to decline from about 127 million in 2003 to about 100 million by 2050. The UN expects an even greater population decline in the Russian Federation, where population is forecast to fall from 145 million in 2003 to 101 million in 2050. In this case, low fertility rates are a consequence of both female education and social unease. It seems likely that the government will try to promote higher fertility rates to avoid such a drastic fall in population.

It seems clear that economic development proceeds more quickly when population growth rates are relatively low. The situation in Asia, home to 60% of the world's population, is especially critical. World Bank figures show that East Asia's GNP grew by an average of 7.4% a year in the period 1965-96, while population was growing at 1.8% a year. During this period, population grew at 2.7% a year in the Middle East and Africa – a rate well ahead of increases in economic output. It is not surprising that these regions are the source of so much political turmoil.

The table (on the next page) shows key indicators for some of the world's biggest and fastest-growing countries. There are some encouraging signs here. Life expectancy, female literacy and purchasing power have risen in most of the countries shown and the average number of children per woman has fallen markedly. Fertility in Iran, where the Islamic government has pursued a highly effective programme of family planning, is only a third of its level in the early 1990s. Note, however, the continuing high rates of fertility in Nigeria, Pakistan and Sierra Leone.

Note also the difference between China, where an authoritarian government has succeeded in doubling living standards and reducing fertility to below 'replacement level', and India, where GDP per head has also doubled but where the government has struggled to improve rates of both fertility and illiteracy.

Some comparative statistics related to the pop

Country (population 2003)	Life expectancy at birth (years)		Adult female literacy %	
	TYP	Latest	TYP	Latest
Algeria *(32 million)*	67	70	46	60
Bangladesh *(147 million)*	53	61	22	26
Brazil *(178 million)*	67	68	80	85
China *(1,304 million)*	70	71	62	73
Egypt *(72 million)*	62	69	34	71
Germany *(82 million)*	76	78	99	99
India *(1,065 million)*	57	64	34	54
Indonesia *(220 million)*	60	67	68	66
Iran *(69 million)*	65	70	43	66
Mexico *(103 million)*	70	73	85	87
Nigeria *(124 million)*	54	51	40	56
Pakistan *(154 million)*	60	61	21	24
Philippines *(80 million)*	64	70	90	94
Sierra Leone *(5 million)*	43	34	11	18
USA *(294 million)*	76	77	99	99

Sources: *Britannica Book of the Year 2004*, United Nations, World Bank, etc.

ulation problem (selected countries)

% of population under 15		Total fertility rate (average children per woman)		Purchasing power parity (per capita 2001)	
TYP	Latest	TYP	Latest	TYP	Latest
44	33	4.2	3.2	$5,640	$5,910
44	38	4.9	3.5	$1,160	$1,600
35	28	3.0	2.2	$5,240	$7,070
28	23	2.0	1.8	$1,680	$3,950
40	35	3.9	3.3	$3,600	$3560
16	15	1.3	1.4	$19,770	$25,240
36	33	3.6	3.0	$1,150	$2,820
37	30	3.0	2.4	$2,730	$2,830
47	32	6.6	2.3	$4,670	$5,940
38	32	3.2	2.5	$3,321	$8,240
45	44	6.5	5.4	$1,360	$790
44	41	6.1	5.1	$1,970	$1,860
39	36	4.1	3.2	$2,440	$4,070
45	44	6.5	6.5	$800	$460
22	21	2.1	2.1	$22,130	$34,280

Latest = Latest available figures   **TYP** = Ten years previously

5 Limiting Population Growth

Efforts to contain population have ranged from coercive sterilisation to voluntary programmes of family planning, health care, education and economic development.

Family planning

Very few women want to spend their reproductive lives pregnant. But for those without effective contraception there may be little choice. Only 60% of the world's women have reliable access to modern family planning services. Making efficient and hygienic contraception available to all is a major objective of governments and international aid agencies.

Fertility rates in Europe and North America used to be just as high as they are now in Africa. But the process of demographic transition has reached the point where populations in many industrialised countries are beginning to decline. This process is now taking place in other parts of the world, sometimes bringing remarkably rapid changes in population growth. It took the US 58 years to reduce average fertility rate from 6.5 children per woman to 3.5. Indonesia achieved the same result in 27 years, while Colombia took 15 years, Thailand eight years and China only seven years.

Improved literacy, better health care, social reform and the use of modern contraception have combined to bring about these dramatic falls in fertility rates. Economic development has no doubt reinforced the trend, but is not enough in itself. Substantial falls in birth rates have been recorded even in very poor countries, such as Brazil and Sri Lanka. Government-led family planning

Use of modern contraceptives

Despite considerable success in spreading the availability of family planning in developing countries, less than 15% of married women in Sub-Saharan Africa use modern contraception (compared with 71% in North America). Large fast-growing countries with low usage rates of modern contraception include Pakistan (17%), Nigeria (9%) and Ethiopia (6%).

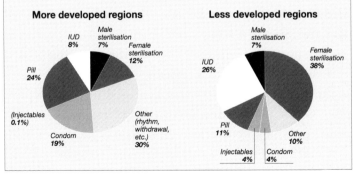

More developed regions

IUD 8%
Male sterilisation 7%
Female sterilisation 12%
Pill 24%
(Injectables 0.1%)
Condom 19%
Other (rhythm, withdrawal, etc.) 30%

Less developed regions

Male sterilisation 7%
Female sterilisation 38%
IUD 26%
Pill 11%
Injectables 4%
Condom 4%
Other 10%

programmes have clearly played an important part in helping countries to limit population growth, although the types and prevalence of different methods of family planning vary greatly from country to country. In Japan, for example, the birth control pill is rarely used, although it is one of the most common forms of contraception in Europe. Voluntary sterilisation (such as vasectomy for men and tubal ligation for women) is common in China and the United States, but relatively rare in southern Europe. Some authorities, overzealous in pursuit of population control, have sanctioned compulsory sterilisation, though this is now rare, thanks to pressure from human rights organisations. Slovakia and Peru, however, were both criticised for allowing forced sterilisation of Romani and Indian women in the 1990s.

Throughout the world, women want more control over their reproductive lives. It is now rare for governments to actively discourage contraception. But lack of availability of modern methods and cultural opposition to contraceptive use (especially in male-dominated societies) are common in many developing countries.

A wide variety of contraceptive methods have been used over the years, ranging from early goatskin sheaths to modern hormonal implants. The Mexican yam, a plant used in traditional birth control remedies, is an important source of the progesterone and oestrogen used in contraceptive pills. Other plant-based birth control methods include pennyroyal, mugwort, acacia gum, date palm, cotton root bark and neem leaves. Traditional herbal remedies such as

Queen Anne's lace or cow parsley appear to work in much the same way as the 'morning-after pill' RU-486 by stopping the production of progesterone and thus the development of a fertilised ovum in the woman's uterus.

As medicine developed in the Western world, traditional methods fell into disrepute. Women who recommended herbal birth control methods were liable to be burnt at the stake for witchcraft. It was not until the 1920s that birth control clinics began to appear, pioneered by Margaret Sanger in the US and Marie Stopes in the UK. In 1951 the newly-independent India became the first country to introduce an official family planning programme. The administration was right to be concerned about the future. Despite a series of population and reproductive health programmes since that time, India's population has tripled, growing from 360 million in 1951 to over a billion in 2003.

Fear of sexually transmitted diseases, and especially HIV/ Aids,[6] has made the condom an increasingly popular form

Population 'control' is out, 'holistic' programmes are in

India has long abandoned compulsory sterilisation in favour of financial incentives to birth control. China still puts pressure on couples to avoid having more than one child. A dramatic drop in birth rates has been achieved in Thailand, thanks to a programme combining education, health care and family planning.

The United Nations Human Development Index (HDI)

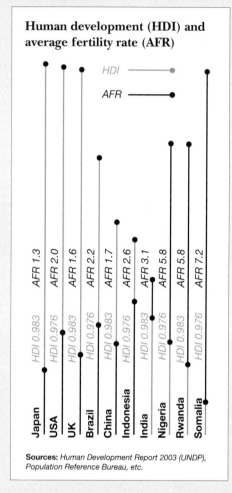

Human development (HDI) and average fertility rate (AFR)

HDI ————●

AFR ————●

Country	AFR	HDI
Japan	AFR 1.3	HDI 0.983
USA	AFR 2.0	HDI 0.976
UK	AFR 1.6	HDI 0.983
Brazil	AFR 2.2	HDI 0.976
China	AFR 1.7	HDI 0.983
Indonesia	AFR 2.6	HDI 0.976
India	AFR 3.1	HDI 0.983
Nigeria	AFR 5.8	HDI 0.976
Rwanda	AFR 5.8	HDI 0.983
Somalia	AFR 7.2	HDI 0.976

Sources: *Human Development Report 2003 (UNDP), Population Reference Bureau, etc.*

The United Nations Human Development Index (HDI), first introduced in 1990, attempts to compare the quality of life in different countries by measuring life expectancy, literacy, and purchasing power. These depend in turn on factors such as standards of health care and education, access to clean water and sanitation, and the size and distribution of GNP. Countries with a high level of human development tend to have low population growth and vice versa. Above is a comparison of HDI and fertility rates for selected countries.

Most common types of contraception used in developing countries

Tubectomy (female sterilisation) – Highly effective (0.2-1% failure rate), one-time procedure, but requires skilled medical practitioner.

Intrauterine device (IUD) – Highly effective (1-6% failure rate), long-term reversible method. Requires trained personnel to fit or remove. Most common type used is copper-T. Almost 60% of IUD users are in China.

Oral contraceptive pill – Highly effective (1-10% failure rate) method, which regulates periods and reduces blood loss, but requires regular supply and the individual discipline of taking pills on specific days.

Vasectomy (male sterilisation) – Highly effective (0.15-1% failure rate), safe one-time procedure, but requires skilled medical practitioner.

Condom – Effective if properly used, but 5-20% failure rate typical in first year. Must be used each time that intercourse occurs. Protects against sexually transmitted disease.

Other modern methods include injections or implants (Norplant, Mirena, Depo Provera, Lunelle, etc.), cervical caps, spermicides, male hormonal contraceptives, morning-after pills, etc. New long-term contraceptives are under development. Note that it can take 5-20 years for new methods to be accepted.

Source: Population Council, World Bank, etc.

of contraception in Europe, North America and Japan. Its use in the developing world, however, is still relatively rare, despite the issue of millions of free condoms by aid organisations such as UNFPA. Many men refuse to use condoms or don't use them properly. Besides, rubber condoms deteriorate if stored too long in tropical climates, their failure rate is relatively high and they are too expensive for general use. Hence the preference for longer-term and more cost-effective solutions such as the copper-T IUD or, in the case of women who already have enough children, sterilisation.

Governments and family planning organisations naturally emphasise 'prevention' by contraception rather than 'cure' by abortion. Nevertheless, safe abortion is regarded by most population experts as a vital part of reproductive health care for women – especially in the developing world where most abortions involve married women who already have several children. RU-486, the abortion pill first introduced in France in the 1980s, was not approved for use in the US until 2000 because of political opposition. Unsafe abortions, performed without proper medical supervision, probably kill 80,000 women a year, 13% of all pregnancy-related deaths worldwide – clearly demonstrating a huge unmet need for family planning.

6 The Status of Women

Improving the education and social status of women in the Third World is crucial to reducing population growth – and to achieving economic development.

Fertility statistics show a direct correlation between female education and birth rates

Many women in the developing world are trapped by poverty or cultural expectations into a lifetime of child-bearing. Many argue that reproductive freedom is the freedom from which all other freedoms flow.

The quality of reproductive health care has a major impact on women's lives. About 600,000 women a year die from complications caused by pregnancy or childbirth. The unavailability of modern contraception, or the lack of choice to suit individual needs, drives many women to use unsuitable or unhygienic methods of birth control. Some 50 million women a year resort to abortion to terminate unwanted pregnancies, with half of them using methods which are illegal and unsafe.

A woman's right to control the functions of her own body[7] is one particularly controversial aspect of the whole population question. But limiting population growth is not simply a matter of giving women reproductive freedom, i.e., the choice as to when and how many times to get pregnant. Many women in developing countries suffer the disadvantages of poverty, ill health, second-class legal status, lack of land and a crushing burden of responsibility for household and family – including growing food and fetching water – as well as bearing children. Women may

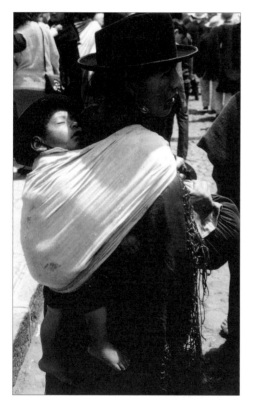

In most of the world, women carry the main burden of caring for children, growing and cooking food, looking after the home and managing family money. Yet women are often treated as second-class citizens, with little or no say in their reproductive rights.

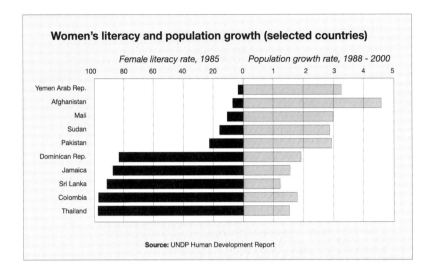

Women's literacy and population growth (selected countries)

Source: UNDP Human Development Report

not be able to own land, inherit property, qualify for credit or loans, or get a decent education. Many jobs are closed to them. In short, they are trapped in a cycle of child-bearing and child-rearing, which may amount to a form of lifelong servitude.

Raising the status of women is partly a question of human rights, but it is increasingly recognised that it is also a crucial aspect of economic development. Societies tend to be more successful and prosperous where women are better educated and can play a full part, alongside men, in organising and managing daily life.

Two states in India symbolise the difference. In Kerala, where women have a high social status, birth and infant mortality rates are low and poverty is declining. In Bihar, where women have low social status, birth and death rates are high and poverty is endemic.

Social and economic development – the key role of women

"A cornerstone of new development thinking is the full integration of women into the mainstream of development and concern for progress in all aspects of their lives – health, education, employment, nutrition, legal and political rights. In traditional development thinking, investment in social development was seen as a luxury, a fruit of economic success. But we now know that the opposite is true: the basis of economic progress is a healthy, socially stable and slow-growing population. Instead of being the fruit of development, social programmes, especially those addressing the status of women, are its very foundation."

Quoted from the welcoming address given by Dr Nafis Sadik, head of the United Nations Population Fund, at the New Delhi population science summit in 1993.

The *machismo* factor

Aggressive masculinity pervades many societies, with men showing off to their friends their prowess in gambling, drinking and controlling women. A typical sign of virility is the number of children a man can father. Physical violence or abandonment is common in societies where women have low social status.

In a *machismo* culture, women may be afraid to seek family planning advice or to use contraception because their husbands become angry if they find out. In theory, couples share responsibility for birth control, but women account for 83% of all contraceptive use worldwide, and men only 17%. Overcoming such cultural blocks to family planning is a serious problem in many parts of the world.

Education is the key

Education is the key to reproductive health and sustainable population growth. In Latin America, as in the Indian states of Bihar, Rajasthan, Madhya Pradesh and Uttar Pradesh, traditional cultural values hold strong. Women have low status and female illiteracy is widespread. Population growth in northern India is twice the national average and well above sustainable levels. India, with its diverse mix of cultures, has been less successful than China

in educating citizens about the desirability of small families. In the Chinese poster shown here, the joys of a one-child family are promoted. To help overcome the traditional preference for sons, these happy parents are shown with a daughter. The picture below shows an outdoor class in Sri Lanka, where a good school system has greatly improved the education of both sexes and contributed to a reduction in average family size over the last 30 years.

7 The World in 2050

Many politicians and religious leaders still fail to see the urgency of the population issue. If future global overload is to be avoided, action is needed now – and must be sustained.

Substantial growth inevitable

Estimates of future population vary from the apocalyptic to the sustainable. It is impossible to be precise about the size of the population even in 50 years time, but the present number of people of reproductive age makes further substantial growth inevitable.

Demographers typically produce a range of estimates based on different assumptions about fertility, mortality, etc. Small differences in the assumptions can result in big differences in actual population. For example, the UN's 'high' projection of world population in 2050 is 12.5 billion people, while its 'medium' projection is 9 billion, and its 'low' 7.8bn. Even at the low level, population would have tripled since 1950.

In late 2003, the UN issued population estimates for 2300, showing that population would reach a staggering 134 trillion if current rates of fertility were maintained until then. Such an outcome is clearly impossible, but the figures show the unsustainability of high fertility rates. Assuming that fertility rates will in fact continue to fall, the UN estimates that population in 2300 will be somewhere between 2.3bn and 36.4bn. The low scenario would only occur if fertility rates remained at 1.85, while the high scenario assumes half a child more per mother (2.35). The 'medium scenario' (based on replacement-level fertility of 2.1) projects that world population will reach a maximum of 9.2bn in 2075, decline to 8.3bn in 2175 and then grow again to 9bn by 2300.

Political commitment to limiting population growth has been half-hearted and controversial. Some governments continue to believe that more people will bring more power and more economic prosperity. Others put their faith in technology – believing that science will come up with new ways to produce food and energy. Some see attempts to limit

Optimists and prophets of doom

Some experts believe that the tide of population growth has already turned. Others warn of global anarchy and environmental disaster caused by massive overcrowding of our small and fragile planet. The next decade will be a critical test of humanity's will to safeguard its own future.

population as an infringement of human rights, especially when it is the rich world lecturing the poor world on the need for birth control. It is still argued, with some justification, that the main environmental threat to the planet is excessive consumption in rich countries, rather than burgeoning population in the developing countries.

In recent years, planners have accepted the need to integrate population policy and development planning. Thus population programmes are increasingly linked to projects aimed at reducing poverty, improving health and education, protecting the environment and, above all, improving the condition of women. In some countries,

Fertility trends 1950 - 2040

In most countries fertility rates are on a downward trend, giving hope that future population may not grow as rapidly as feared. But the high proportion of young people in the present population provides a built-in momentum of growth. A fertility rate of 2.1 is regarded as replacement level.

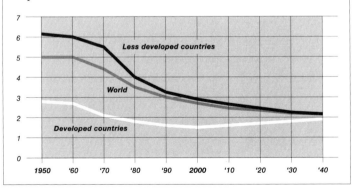

religious fundamentalism conflicts with moves to extend women's rights and reproductive freedom. Although a major study by the distinguished Muslim scholar Professor Abdel Rahim Omran concluded that modern family planning is acceptable to the great majority of Islamic theologians, some traditionalists oppose the notion of equal rights for women. This is an important issue in view of the fact that Muslims make up a quarter of world population.

The Roman Catholic Church, led by Pope John Paul II, has opposed abortion and all forms of artificial contraception, arguing that fears of a population explosion are unfounded and alarmist. At the 1994 UN population conference in Cairo, the Vatican and ten Roman Catholic states, together with a few Muslim countries, refused to endorse the complete text of an international action plan designed to tackle the population problem. Yet the Roman Catholic church is active in supporting education and health care programmes, and many individual Catholics give close support to family planning clinics at local level.

The attitude of the US government is also important. There is a strong anti-abortion movement in the US and, in 1973, Senator Jesse Helms pushed through a law banning the use of US money for abortions or forced sterilisations. At the 1984 UN population conference in Mexico City, President Reagan announced that US aid would no longer be permitted to go to NGOs that were involved in voluntary abortion activities, even if such activities were undertaken with non-US funds. The result was a surge in abortions

Key factors in moving towards sustainable world population

Education
Education, especially for women, is probably the best contraceptive of all.

Health care
People tend to have smaller families when they can be sure that most of their children will survive and grow up healthy.

Family planning
Women in most societies want easily accessible, safe and affordable contraception.

Economic development
Increased economic prosperity is usually accompanied by a fall in birth rates.

Social development
Alleviating poverty, improving the social status of women and changing cultural pressures towards large families would all contribute to lower population growth.

International aid
The developing countries (where 95% of population growth is taking place) need technical and financial help to meet population objectives.

Consumer habits
If population growth is not to destroy the environment, society needs to abandon the wasteful habits of consumerism and move towards a sustainable approach.

Budgeting for survival

Even with declining fertility rates, world population is
likely to increase by 50% in the next 50 years. It could be
very much higher if population programmes fail. Family
planning services could be extended to everyone in the
world for less than $20bn a year – roughly the amount
that Americans spend on pet food.

worldwide as funding for family planning fell away. The
'Mexico City restrictions' were repealed by President
Clinton and the 1990s saw a reduction in rates of both
population growth and abortion at worldwide level. As
soon as George W. Bush took office in 2001, however, he
issued an executive memo stopping US federal support
for any programme that permitted abortion.

Unlike capital spending on sanitation or schools, the
benefits of money spent on population programmes only
show up after decades of effort. Thus political support
is hard to muster. According to Thoraya Ahmed Obaid,
Executive Director of UNFPA, "international funding
for population and reproductive health programmes
is just 40% of what was agreed upon by governments
in 1994 at the International Conference on Population
and Development in Cairo". Yet, as a World Bank report
pointed out, "family planning investments actually save
money. Reduced maternal and child health care costs
create short-term savings that often amount to double
the cost of the family planning programme; additional
savings accrue as lower fertility eases the demands on

the education system". In short, family planning is a key aspect of development.

Meanwhile, the gap between rich and poor is growing both between and within individual countries. With the concentration of huge numbers of poor people in cities, the potential for radicalisation is obvious. Concern about population growth is entwined with worries about the political stability as well as the environmental health of our fragile planet.

Additional notes

1 neo-Malthusian

Thomas Malthus was both mathematician and priest. In 1798 he published his famous work "An Essay on the Principle of Population". The essay postulated that the disparity between the potential geometrical growth rate of population and the arithmetical growth rate of food supply presented humanity with a stark choice between population control and ultimate starvation. Malthus' discussion of the checks on population growth led Darwin to develop his "survival of the fittest" theory to explain the origin of species.

2 abortion

Worldwide, an estimated 40-60 million abortions take place each year, 40% of them in illegal and often unsafe conditions. Without proper medical care, abortions can be very dangerous. Many thousands of women die each year from 'back-street' abortions. In recent decades, more and more governments have accepted that the provision of safe and legal abortion should be an integral part of reproductive health services for women.

According to a UN review of abortion policies worldwide, published in June 2002, abortion is legal in most countries, but the grounds on which it is permitted vary greatly. The most common grounds are to preserve the woman's life (98% of countries); to preserve the woman's physical health (63%)

or mental health (62%); in cases of rape or incest (43%) or foetal impairment (39 %); for economic or social reasons (33%); or simply on request (27% – comprising 65% of developed countries but only 14% of developing countries).

The Vatican and the Christian Right in America are strongly opposed to abortion and a bitter controversy has raged between the 'pro-life' and 'pro-choice' camps. Abortion was legalised in the US in 1973 (in *Roe v. Wade*) and, despite numerous legal challenges, has remained so. About 1.3 million legal abortions are performed in the United States each year. The re-election in late-2004 of President Bush, strongly supported by the Christian Right, increased the possibility of changes in the Supreme Court that could lead to the overturning of the *Roe* decision and the removal of a woman's right to abortion in the US.

3 The Black Death

The bubonic plague which ravaged Europe in the mid-14th century is thought to have killed 25 million people – a third of the population of medieval Europe. Will the concentration of people in urban areas and the emergence of drug-resistant strains of bacteria and viruses eventually create a modern version of the plague? The outbreak of SARS in 2003 may have been a harbinger of pandemics to come.

4 biodiversity

The destruction of animal and plant habitats has escalated at frightening rates during the 20th century. Estimates of species loss vary greatly, but it is clear that huge numbers of insects, birds, fish, mammals and plants are in danger of extinction as habitats are disturbed by expanding human settlements and resource use. Some experts believe the world is facing the biggest species loss since the events which wiped out the dinosaurs some 65 million years ago.

The international Convention on Biodiversity, signed at the Rio Earth Summit in 1992, was a first step towards preventing habitat loss. However, the effectiveness of the Convention depends on the willingness of governments to translate words into action.

5 demographic transition

When death rates go down, there is a time lag before birth rates also decline. It may take many years before sufficient cultural changes take place to make smaller families the norm, turning rapid population growth into zero growth or even decline. This process, sparked by industrialisation and economic development, is known as demographic transition.

6 HIV/Aids

It is sometimes suggested that Aids will provide a natural curb on population growth in poor countries. HIV/Aids is a terrible scourge, predicted to cause 278 million deaths in the period 2000-2050 – and 178 million fewer births because of mothers made ill by the disease. The biggest impact will be in Sub-Saharan Africa where HIV/Aids has high rates of prevalence. Yet, even taking into account the effect of HIV/Aids, Africa's population is predicted to grow from 851 million in 2003 to between 1.5bn and 2.1bn in 2050, because of relatively high fertility rates.

The UN's 2002 revision of population forecasts looked at 53 of the worst-hit countries – which account for 93% of all worldwide HIV-infected adults – and found that population would probably be reduced only in countries with HIV prevalence rates over 20%, i.e., in Botswana, South Africa, Lesotho and Swaziland. The impact of HIV/Aids on the developing world will be devastating, since the disease is most prevalent among the younger and most productive members of society. The cost of having huge numbers of people, ill from Aids or working to look after Aids patients, is likely to wreck hopes of economic development in some countries.

7 breastfeeding

The encouragement of breastfeeding has two aspects as far as population is concerned. First, it provides infants with safe and nourishing food (usually preferable to powdered babyfoods which can be lethal unless used with clean water). Second, it helps as a natural contraceptive, since the return to fertility is delayed during the lactation period.

Some technical terms

Birth and Death Rates (often referred to as "crude rates") are expressed as the number of births or deaths per thousand people in the population and do not take into account age structure. Although health care in richer countries is much better than in the Third World, crude death rates may be higher because developed countries have a larger proportion of elderly people.

Rate of Natural Increase (RNI) Birth rate minus the death rate, i.e., the rate of annual population growth, disregarding the impact of migration and expressed as a percentage.

Population doubling time, based upon RNI, is the number of years taken to double the population, assuming a constant rate of natural increase. Like all straight line extrapolations, doubling times have to be treated with caution.

Infant Mortality Rate The annual number of deaths of infants under the age of one year per thousand live births.

Total Fertility Rate (TFR) The average number of children a woman would bear, assuming a continuation of current birth rates.

Life Expectancy at Birth The average number of years a newborn infant can be expected to live, assuming a continuation of current mortality levels.

Bibliography

Sources

Periodicals, organisations, etc.

All-Party Parliamentary Group on Population, Development and Reproductive Health (UK); Interact Worldwide (formerly Population Concern); "The Coming Anarchy", an article by Robert D. Kaplan in *The Atlantic Monthly*, February 1994; Family Planning Association of India; Government of India; *The Economist*; *Human Development Report 2004*, UNDP; *The Independent;* International Conference on Population and Development, Cairo 1994; International Planned Parenthood Federation; *Living Planet Report 2002*, WWF; Marie Stopes International; Oxfam; *People & the Planet;* Population Concern; *The Times*; World Bank; World Conservation Union; *World Population Prospects: The 2002 Revision*, UN; Womankind Worldwide, *World Resources 2002-2004*, World Resources Institute.

Books

Population: *The Complex Reality*, ed. by Sir Frances Graham-Smith, the Royal Society and North American Press, 1994 (404 pages; ISBN 0-85403-484-6)

A collection of 25 papers presented at the Population Summit of the world's scientific academies held in New Delhi in 1993.

The conference issued a 'Population Statement', signed by 60 of the scientific academies which participated, pointing out that even the most optimistic scenarios of lower birth rates lead to a peak of some 8 billion people by 2050. Meanwhile food production from both land and sea declined relative to world population growth in the previous decade. The achievement of social, economic and personal well-being and protection of the environment means that "we must achieve zero population growth within the lifetime of our children". Achieving this goal requires equal opportunities for women and men in sexual, social and economic life, universal access to convenient family planning and health services, clean water, sanitation, primary health care and education, appropriate governmental policies and "a new ethic that eschews wasteful consumption".

Population Matters: *Demographic change, economic growth and poverty in the developing world*, edited by Nancy Birsall, Allen C. Kelley and Steven Sinding, Oxford University Press, 2003 (456 pages; ISBN 0-19926-186-5)

A collection of essays analysing the link between family planning and economic prosperity. The question as to whether rapid population growth stimulates or hampers economic progress is discussed in detail by a range of experts. Based on evidence from developing countries in the 1980s and 1990s, it appears that countries with high rates of population growth have tended to see less economic growth.

The End of World Population Growth: *Human capital and sustainable development in the 21st century,* ed. by Wolfgang Lutz and W. Sanderson, Earthscan, 2004
(304 pages; ISBN 0-84407-089-1)

A look at current demographic trends. On the one hand are the populations which have stabilised and show an increasing proportion of older people. On the other hand are those countries where fertility rates remain above replacement level and population is continuing to grow apace. While the 20th century was a period of rapid population growth, the 21st century seems likely to see stabilisation of total population accompanied by rapid ageing.

World Population, Turning the Tide: *Three decades of progress,* by Stanley P. Johnson, published by Graham & Trotman/ Martinus Nijhoff, 1994
(387 pages; ISBN 1-85966-047-9)

A history of the international community's efforts to get to grips with the population problem from the 1960s to the 1990s. The text is supplemented by many demographic tables and graphs. The book tracks the emergence of a global consensus that population change, poverty, inequality, patterns of consumption and threats to the environment are so closely connected that none of them can be considered in isolation. Johnson strikes a relatively optimistic note, pointing to the success of many countries in reducing population growth rates and fertility in recent years.

Other relevant publications

Commitments: Youth reproductive health, the World Bank and the Millennium Development Goals, Global Health Council, 2004;

An Overcrowded World: Population, resources and the environment, edited by Philip Sarre and John Blunden, Oxford UP, 1995;

World Population and Fertility Planning Technologies: The next 20 years, Office of Technology Assessment, US Congress, Univ. Press of the Pacific, 2003;

21st Century Debates: An overcrowded world? Rob Bowden, Hodder Wayland, 2003;

The Return of Malthus: Environmentalism and post-war population-resources crises, Bjorn-Ola Linner, White Horse Press, 2003;

The Rapid Growth of Human Populations 1750 - 2000, by Dr William Stanton, Multi-Science Publishing, 2003;

Cities Transformed: Demographic change and its implications in the developing world, ed. Mark R. Montgomery et al., Earthscan, 2003;

Politics and Population Control, by Kathleen A. Tobin, Greenwood Press, 2004;

Do Family Planning Services Affect Abortion?, Julie S. DaVanzo and Clifford Grammich, RAND Corporation, 2004;

Demographic Influences on Water Resources, Jill Boberg, RAND Corporation, 2004;

State of the World 2002, Worldwatch Institute;

The Skeptical Environmentalist, by Bjorn Lomborg, Cambridge UP, 2001;

The Third Revolution: Environment, population and a sustainable world, by Paul Harrison, I.B. Tauris & Co. Ltd., 1992;

Population and Development in Poor Countries: Selected essays, by Julian L. Simon and others, Princeton University Press, 1992;

The Population Explosion, by Paul and Anne Ehrlich, Arrow Books, 1991;

An Essay on the Principle of Population, by Thomas Malthus, 1798.

Useful websites

un.org/popin – UN Population Information Network, UN Department of Economic and Social Affairs, Population Division

unfpa.org – UN Population Fund

prb.org – Population Reference Bureau

popcouncil.org – Population Council

populationaction.org – Population Action

ippf.org – International Planned Parenthood Federation

populationinstitute.org – Population Institute

agi-usa.org – Alan Guttmacher Institute

pop.org – Population Research Institute

rifpd.org – Rotarian Initiative for Population and Development

worldwatch.org – Worldwatch Institute

appg-popdevrh.org.uk – All Party Parliamentary Group on Population, Development and Reproductive Health

populationconcern.org.uk – Interact Worldwide (formerly Population Concern)

globalforumhealth.org – Global Forum for Health

peopleandplanet.net – internet gateway for population, poverty, health, consumption and the environment (sponsored by UNFPA, IUCN, WWF, etc.)

World Population

maps, charts and statistics

Sources *Britannica Book of the Year 2004*; Population
Reference Bureau; United Nations (Department of
Economic and Social Affairs, Population Division), etc.

UGI Report 122

Population density
(inhabitants per square kilometre)

The map shows population density by country. It should be remembered that density may vary greatly within a single country. Thus most of Australia's population is concentrated around its western rim and 96% of Egyptians live in the Nile Valley.

Apart from 'city states' such as Singapore and Hong Kong (over 6,000 people per sq km), small islands and enclaves such as the Gaza Strip (where density is close to 3,500), the countries with the highest population density are Bangladesh (904), Taiwan (620), South Korea (479), The Netherlands (389), Lebanon (353), Belgium (337), Japan (337), India (331) and Israel (313).

Figure 1: Population by density

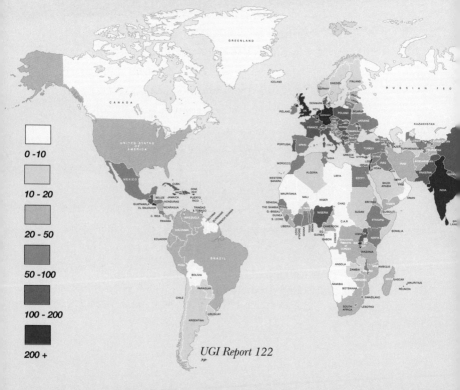

0 -10

10 - 20

20 - 50

50 -100

100 - 200

200 +

UGI Report 122

Countries with a very low density of population include Namibia and Mongolia (2), Australia, Botswana, Canada and Mauritania (3) and Angola (8). The population density of the world's largest countries varies markedly. Examples include China (134), the US (31), Brazil (21), Sudan (15), the Russian Federation (8) and Kazakhstan (5).

Water resources and land fertility have an obvious bearing on the capacity of a particular region to support a large population, but other factors are involved too. Thus Kuwait has no water resources of its own, but has substantial reserves of oil which can be traded to purchase food and water. Similarly Hong Kong would be quite unable to sustain its population from home-grown food, but its ability to earn money through financial services and trade has enabled its population to survive and grow.

Large parts of the globe are unsuitable for human settlement because of mountains, jungle, ice or desert. The limitations of climate and topography put additional pressure on those areas which offer better living conditions. If ways could be found to clothe arid areas with vegetation – a dream of many planners in the Middle East and Africa – it would provide extra living space for fast-growing populations.

But technology – even with massive and costly water transfer projects – has been only modestly successful in turning deserts green. Water shortages are particularly acute in the Middle East where population density is already high – and growing.

Between 2003 and 2050, population is expected to double in Yemen, Saudi Arabia, Kuwait, Iraq, Jordan, Oman and the Palestinian territories. Israel's population is predicted to grow from 6.7 million to 11 million by 2050. Disputes over water resources can be expected to intensify. Land shortages caused by high population density in Rwanda (293 people per sq km) and Burundi (246) contributed to the pressures that spawned genocide and war in the 1990s.

The geopolitical balance

The pie charts compare the make-up of world population between 'developed' countries and 'developing' countries in Asia, Africa and Latin America. In 1950 the richer developed

Figure 2: The changing geopolitical balance

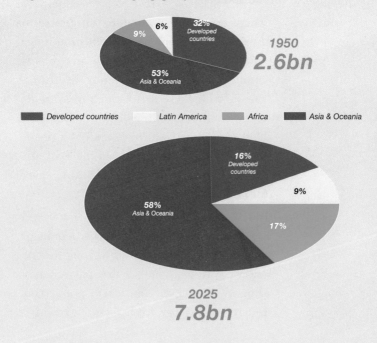

1950
2.6bn

Developed countries   Latin America   Africa   Asia & Oceania

32% Developed countries
6%
9%
53% Asia & Oceania

16% Developed countries
9%
17%
58% Asia & Oceania

2025
7.8bn

countries of the world accounted for about a third of total world population, with developing countries accounting for two-thirds. By 2025 the proportion of people living in developed countries will have been halved and the great majority of the world's population will be living in developing countries.

It should be noted that the distinction between 'developed' and 'developing' countries is becoming more and more blurred. In practice, 'developed' tends to imply membership of the OECD. Some developing countries, such as India and China, show enormous regional disparity, with parts having the character of modern industrialised societies and others which remain traditional rural communities.

The growing gap between the relatively small number of 'rich' people and the huge mass of the poor creates political tensions in many countries. These tensions are bound to increase as population growth further swells the number of urban poor.

Total estimated population

Nearly 60% of the world's people live in Asia but by far the fastest rate of population growth is taking place in Africa. By 2025 Africa is expected to account for 17% of total world population (up from 12% in 1994 and only 9% in 1950).

Total world population is increasing at over 75 million people a year and some 95% of the growth is taking place in developing countries. In Europe, by contrast, population is declining and is likely to be affected much more by migration than by natural increases.

Most East European countries have seen a natural decline in population in recent years while others have had only

Figure 3: Total estimated population

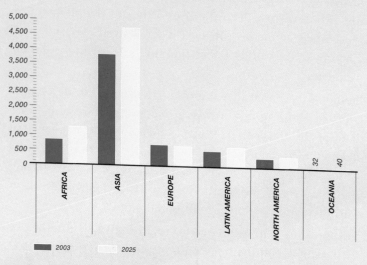

2003 □ 2025

marginal increases. Europe's fastest-growing country is Albania (1.1% a year). Germany with a rate of -0.1% contrasts with France (+0.4%), the UK (+0.1%) and Italy (-0.1%). The rate of natural increase in Europe as a whole is -0.1% compared with +2.2% in Africa, +1.4% in Latin America and the Caribbean, and +1.3% in Asia.

World's biggest countries in 1950, 2000 and 2050

In 1950 the world's ten most populous countries were China (555m) India (358m), the US (158m), Russia (103m), Japan (84m), Indonesia (79m), Germany (68m), Brazil (54m), the UK (50m) and Italy (47m). By 2050 the ten largest countries are expected to be India (1,531m), China (1,395m), US (409m), Pakistan (349m), Indonesia (294m), Nigeria (259m), Bangladesh (255m), Brazil (233m), Ethiopia (171m) and

Figure 4: World's biggest countries in 1950, 2000 and 2050

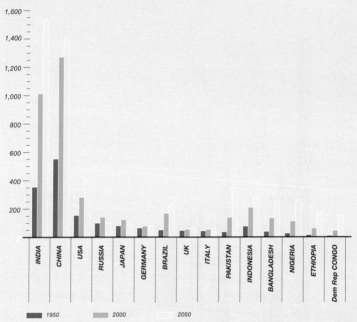

the Democratic Republic of the Congo (152m). The UK, long ranked as one of the world's biggest countries in terms of population (9th in 1950), is expected to rank only 26th by 2050. Meanwhile, the DRC (the former Zaire), is forecast to change from being a small country of 12 million in 1950 to the world's tenth largest state in 2050.

Annual population growth

Population growth is declining as the process of demographic transition takes place, but the rates of decline vary considerably. Africa's population is growing at almost twice the rate of Asia's. However, although the growth rate in

Figure 5: Estimated annual population growth

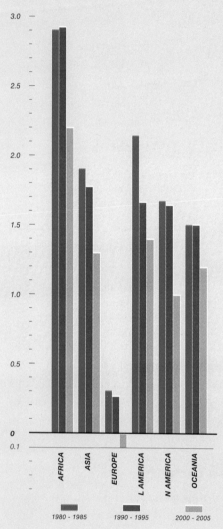

3.0

2.5

2.0

1.5

1.0

0.5

0

0.1

AFRICA ASIA EUROPE L AMERICA N AMERICA OCEANIA

1980 - 1985   1990 - 1995   2000 - 2005

Asia is estimated at only 1.3% for the period 2000-2005, the large size of the base population implies a yearly addition of about 50 million people, compared with about 19 million a year in Africa. In Europe, natural population growth has ended and been replaced with a slight decline. Europe's population is expected to fall from 725m in 2003 to 632m in 2050.

Perhaps the biggest demographic change that is taking place is population ageing. In 1950 the median age of the world's population was 23.6 years. This had risen to 26.4 by 2000 and is expected to reach 36.8 years in 2050 (47.7 in Europe, 27.5 in Africa) and about 48 years by 2300.

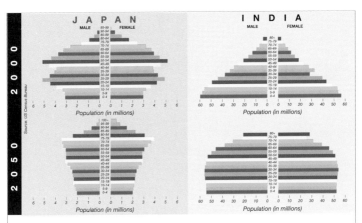

Source: US Census Bureau

The age structure of population

A population which includes a large number of young people approaching reproductive age has a built-in momentum towards growth. In the developing world, 36% of the population is under 15. The world now has over a billion teenagers, most of them sexually active – and ill-informed about contraception. Of course, this number of young people also represents a vast potential market for consumer products.

The social implications of age structure are profound too. A disproportionate number of young or old people in the population may put an intolerable burden on those who are in work and who have to pay for education, health care, pensions, etc.

Shown here are age structure diagrams for Japan and India. India's profile in 2000 shows the classic pyramid shape of a fast-growing 'young' population. Japan by contrast reveals a preponderance of people in their middle years. By 2050 Japan will have more old than young people, while India's age groups will have evened out. Note that India's population is ten times that of Japan.

An ageing population is not just a Japanese or European problem. By 2006, India's population will include 86 million people aged 60 or more. Even in India, where family and kinship ties are strong, the forces of urbanisation and modernisation are increasing the vulnerability of the old.

Long-term UN forecasts estimate that, by 2300, the world's population will include 1.5 billion people aged 80 or more, while the median age of the global population will have increased from 26 (18 in Africa)   in 2000 to 48 (46 in Africa) in 2300.

About *UGI* Reports

As the world's population grows, and more nations seek their place in the sun, so the big issues become ever bigger and more complex. And whether in the classroom, in business or just as concerned citizens at the ballot box, the need for reliable, unbiased information, presented in a readable, jargon-free way, has never been greater. Since 1992 that has been the mission of *Understanding Global Issues.*

In a world of instant analysis and 'information overload', *UGI* draws on the best and most up-to-date writings and research on each topic to create an in-depth yet easy-to-read, concise yet thorough, overview of all the key facts and arguments. In the past 12 years *UGI* has published almost 130 Briefings in a periodical format intended mainly for the educational sector.

Now *UGI* Reports takes the most recent topics, revises them where necessary, and presents them in pocket book format for the general reader.

Details of the other five titles in the first batch are given in the following pages. A second batch of six titles is in preparation.

Up-to-date information on the *UGI* publishing programme is always available on www.global-issues.co.uk

World Trade

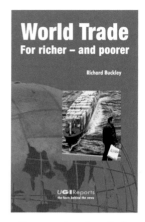

For richer – and poorer

Though the WTO is much reviled by the
anti-globalisation movement, it provides
a powerful framework for beneficial
changes to the global trading system and
hence a real chance to defeat poverty
in developing countries. In a world of
great inequalities, a rules-based system
of international trade is much better than its 'law-of-the-jungle'
alternative. We look at the facts behind the controversies over 'unfair
trade'.

In this UGI Report

The WTO – agent of greed or distribution of wealth?

Trade and History: from colonialism to globalisation

What Is Traded Where: everything from commodities to services

Masters and Slaves: raw materials and industrial society

The Big Trading Blocs: the EU, NAFTA and others

The Regulation of Trade: the WTO, GATT, GATS and TRIPS

Barriers to Trade: low tariffs and high hurdles

Trade and Development: export or die

Additional notes

Bibliography

Maps, charts and statistics

UGI Report 122

The IMF & World Bank

Funding a better future?

The IMF and World Bank were founded after World War II, with the twin objectives of reconstructing a devastated Europe, and establishing a global financial framework to guard against the economic depression and social breakdown which many thought had led to war in the first place. This briefing examines how well these aims were achieved, what mistakes have been made, and how these institutions are adapting to a more globalised world.

In this UGI Report

Do They Matter?: public versus private finance

History and Change: from Bretton Woods to the Washington Consensus

The Development Agenda: reversing the growth of poverty

The Debt Burden: the moral dilemmas

Making Things Better: ideas for reform

Widening the Options: regional and local alternative finance

Globalisation Revisited: harnessing the future

Additional notes

Bibliography

Maps, charts and statistics

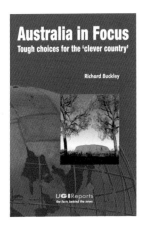

Australia in Focus

Tough choices for the 'clever country'

Australia has undergone radical changes in the last 20 years, embracing both globalisation and multi-ethnic immigration. Traditional strengths in farming and mining have been extended into high-tech manufacturing, financial services, software, tourism, sport – and call centres. Meanwhile, political divisions have sharpened and environmental stress has increased. We take a fresh look at the island continent.

In this UGI Report

Past changes and new challenges in Australia

The First Inhabitants: Aborigines then and now

Anglos, Americans, Asians: from colonialism to globalisation

Economic Realities: from commodities to services

Treasures of the Earth: producing raw materials for industrial society

Red Centre, Green Edge: pressures on a fragile land

The Tyranny of Distance: transport and communications

A Multicultural Society: immigration, population and technology

Additional notes

Bibliography

Maps, charts and statistics

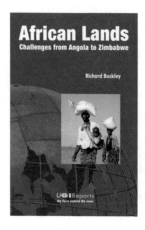

African Lands

Challenges from Angola to Zimbabwe

Optimists talk of an "African Renaissance" with good governance and economic development combining to make life better for the world's poorest continent. Others despair at the chaos, bloodshed and corruption that are still common in many parts of Africa. With its oil industry growing fast and globalisation spreading to the 'dark continent', we look at some of the main factors that will determine success or failure in Sub-Saharan Africa.

In this UGI Report

Big potential, massive task

The Colonial Inheritance: awkward frontiers, alien laws

Styles of Government: African tyranny, African democracy

The Land Tenure Problem: white owners, black aspirations

African Agriculture: large commercial farms, small subsistence plots

From Diamonds to Coltan: the struggle to control resources

The Challenge of Change: governance, corruption and poverty

Africa in the 21st Century: technology and prosperity – for some

Additional notes

Bibliography

Maps, charts and statistics

UGI Report 122

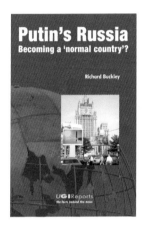

Putin's Russia

Becoming a 'normal country'?

Since 2000, Russia has stabilised under the disciplined leadership of Vladimir Putin, who in March 2004 was re-elected for a second four-year term. Russia's economy has been growing at over 5% a year, mainly thanks to oil, and life is improving for most ordinary people. But the war in Chechnya continues, poverty afflicts 30 million Russians and there are growing concerns over democratic rights. What kind of country is Putin's Russia?

In this UGI Report

A new Russia – with some old habits

Yeltsin Chaos, Putin Order: the stabilisation of Russia

Governing the Federation: eighty-nine units, one Kremlin

An Economic Surge at Last: thanks to oil and gas

Babushkas and Oligarchs: thirty million poor – and 25 billionaires

Environmental Distress: damage done by communism – and the free market

The Military and Chechnya: too many generals, too little cash

Russia's Place in the World: the Eurasian powerhouse

Additional notes

Bibliography

Maps, charts and statistics